stir-fry

simple and delicious easy-to-make recipes

Rachael Philipps

p

This is a Parragon Publishing Book
First published in 2002

Parragon Publishing
Queen Street House
4 Queen Street
Bath, BA1 1HE, UK

ISBN: 0-75258-898-2

Printed in China

Produced by the Bridgewater Book Company Ltd.

Photographer Ian Parsons

Home Economist Sara Hesketh

NOTES FOR THE READER

- This book uses both imperial and metric measurements. Follow the same units of measurement throughout; do not mix imperial and metric.

- All spoon measurements are level: teaspoons are assumed to be 5 ml, and tablespoons are assumed to be 15 ml.

- Unless otherwise stated, milk is assumed to be whole milk, eggs and individual vegetables such as carrots are medium, and pepper is freshly ground black pepper.

- Recipes using raw eggs should be avoided by infants, the elderly, pregnant women, convalescents, and anyone suffering from an illness.

- The times given are an approximate guide only. Preparation times differ according to the techniques used by different people and the cooking times may also vary from those given. Optional ingredients, variations, or serving suggestions have not been included in the calculations.

contents

introduction

Stir-fries are generally fast, tasty, and highly nutritious meals. Only small quantities of meat are used compared with traditional Western cooking, and the healthy emphasis on vegetables, together with accompanying rice and noodles, means they are good for you, too.

Stir-frying is ideal for the busy cook—most recipes are very easy to prepare and quick to cook. And you can be guaranteed to find something in this book to please all tastes, with a wide range of recipes from the Far East, some with Chinese influence and others with spicy Thai and Indian derivation.

The recipes have been divided into four sections—Chicken & Turkey, Fish & Seafood, Beef & Pork, and Vegetables—for ease of reference. You will find that once your confidence grows in this style of cooking, you will enjoy experimenting with ingredients (for example, substituting one kind of meat for another) to suit your own personal tastes.

Stir-frying is a highly versatile and adaptable style of cooking that is great for the bold and imaginative cook. Experiment and enjoy!

guide to recipe key		
	easy	Recipes are graded as follows: 1 pea = easy; 2 peas = very easy; 3 peas = extremely easy.
	serves 4	Recipes generally serve four people. Simply halve the ingredients to serve two, taking care not to mix imperial and metric measurements.
	10 minutes	Preparation time. Where marinating or soaking noodles are involved, these times have been added on separately: eg, 15 minutes + 30 minutes to marinate.
	10 minutes	Cooking time. Cooking times don't include the cooking of rice or noodles served with the main dishes.

hot & spicy chicken with peanuts
page 20

ginger shrimp with oyster mushrooms
page 28

thai marinated beef with celery
page 66

squash & zucchini stir-fry
page 80

chicken
& turkey

Chicken and turkey offer healthy meat options and are very tasty in a wide range of stir-fry dishes—from Curried Turkey with Celery to Chicken with Shiitake Mushrooms. Included in this section are some traditional favorites, such as Chicken Fried Rice, to some more exotic recipes for the bolder cook, such as Turkey with Bamboo Shoots and Water Chestnuts.

curried turkey
with celery

		ingredients	
	very easy	1–2 tbsp vegetable oil	1 orange or red bell pepper,
		13 oz/375 g cooked turkey, cubed	sliced thinly
		1½ tsp medium curry powder	1 tbsp cornstarch
	serves 4	1 tbsp soy sauce	generous 1½ cups water
		2 leeks, sliced thinly	
		4 celery stalks, chopped finely	2 tbsp chopped fresh cilantro,
	10 minutes	2¼ cups snow peas, trimmed	to garnish
		1 yellow bell pepper, sliced thinly	
			cooked noodles or rice, to serve
	8 minutes		

Heat a non-stick wok or skillet and add the oil. Add the turkey, curry powder, soy sauce, and leeks and cook for about 2 minutes, or until the turkey is heated through.

Add the celery, snow peas, and bell peppers. Stir-fry for another 3–4 minutes.

While the vegetables are cooking, dissolve the cornstarch in the water and whisk until well combined. Add the mixture to the stir-fry and cook, stirring constantly until the liquid just thickens.

Remove from the heat and pile over a bed of noodles or rice. Garnish with cilantro and serve immediately.

turkey, broccoli & bok choy

		ingredients	
very easy	MARINADE	1 head of broccoli, cut into florets
	1 tbsp soy sauce	2 heads of bok choy, leaves washed
serves 4	1 tbsp honey	and separated (or savoy cabbage,
	2 cloves garlic, crushed	if bok choy is unavailable)
		1 red bell pepper, sliced thinly
10 minutes + 2 hours to marinate	STIR-FRY	¼ cup chicken bouillon
	1 lb/450 g turkey breast,	
	cut into strips	cooked rice, to serve
9 minutes	1 tbsp vegetable oil	

In a medium-sized bowl, stir together the soy sauce, honey, and garlic. Add the turkey and toss to coat. Cover the bowl with plastic wrap and refrigerate for 2 hours to marinate.

Put a wok or large skillet over a medium–high heat and add the oil; heat for 1 minute. Add the turkey and stir-fry for 3 minutes, or until the turkey is opaque. Remove with a slotted spoon, then set aside and keep warm.

Add the broccoli, bok choy (or savoy cabbage), and bell peppers to the wok and stir-fry for 2 minutes. Add the bouillon and continue to stir-fry for 2 minutes, or until the vegetables are crisp yet tender.

Return the turkey to the pan and cook briefly to reheat. Serve immediately over a bed of hot rice.

lemon turkey
with spinach

		ingredients
	very easy	**MARINADE** · 6 scallions, sliced finely
		1 tbsp soy sauce · ½ lemon, peeled and sliced thinly
	serves 4	1 tbsp white wine vinegar · 1 garlic clove, chopped finely
		1 tsp cornstarch · 10½ oz/300 g spinach, washed,
		1 tsp finely grated lemon zest · drained, and chopped coarsely
	12 minutes	½ tsp finely ground black pepper · 3 tbsp chopped fresh flatleaf parsley
	+30 minutes	· lemon slices, to garnish
	to marinate	**STIR-FRY** · sprigs of flatleaf parsley, to garnish
		1 lb/450 g turkey breast,
	8 minutes	cut into strips · 1 lb 2 oz/500 g cooked tagliatelle or
		1 tbsp vegetable oil · fettucine, to serve

Put the soy sauce, vinegar, cornstarch, lemon zest, and pepper in a bowl and mix thoroughly. Add the turkey and stir to coat. Cover with plastic wrap and marinate in the refrigerator for 30 minutes.

Heat the oil in a large wok or skillet. Add the turkey and the marinade and cook over a medium heat for 2–3 minutes, or until the turkey is opaque.

Add the scallions, lemon slivers, and garlic and cook for another 2–3 minutes. Stir in the spinach and parsley and cook until the spinach is just wilted.

Remove from the heat and spoon over the hot pasta, then garnish with lemon slices and sprigs of parsley before serving.

chicken with pistachio nuts

		ingredients	
very easy		¼ cup chicken bouillon	1 lb/450 g mushrooms, sliced thinly
		2 tbsp soy sauce	1 head of broccoli, cut into florets
serves 4		2 tbsp dry sherry	5½ oz/150 g beansprouts
		3 tsp cornstarch	3½ oz/100 g canned water chestnuts,
		1 egg white, beaten	drained and sliced thinly
15 minutes		½ tsp salt	generous 1 cup pistachio nuts, plus
		4 tbsp peanut or vegetable oil	extra to garnish (optional)
		1 lb/450 g chicken breast,	
9 minutes		cut into strips	boiled white rice, to serve

Combine the chicken bouillon, soy sauce, and sherry with
1 teaspoon of cornstarch. Stir well and set aside.

Combine the egg white, salt, 2 tablespoons of the oil, and
2 teaspoons of cornstarch. Toss the chicken in the mixture to coat.

In a wok or skillet, heat the remaining vegetable oil until hot. Add
the chicken in batches and stir-fry until golden. Remove from the
wok and drain on paper towels, then set aside to keep warm.

Add more oil to the wok if needed and stir-fry the mushrooms,
then add the broccoli and cook for 2–3 minutes.

Return the chicken to the wok and add the beansprouts, water
chestnuts, and pistachio nuts. Stir-fry until all the ingredients are
thoroughly warm. Add the chicken bouillon mixture and cook,
stirring continuously until thickened.

Serve immediately over a bed of rice, garnished with pistachios.

ginger chicken with toasted sesame seeds

		ingredients	
extremely easy		MARINADE	2 carrots, sliced thinly
		4 tbsp soy sauce	½ cauliflower, cut into small florets
serves 4		4 tbsp water	1 tsp grated fresh root ginger
			5 tbsp white wine
		STIR-FRY	2 tbsp sesame seeds
10 minutes + 1 hour to marinate		1 lb 2 oz/500 g chicken breasts, skinned, cut into strips	1 tbsp cornstarch
		2 tbsp peanut oil	1 tbsp water
		1 leek, sliced thinly	
9 minutes		1 head of broccoli, cut into small florets	cooked rice, to serve

In a medium dish, combine the soy sauce with 4 tablespoons of water. Toss and coat the chicken strips in the sauce. Cover the dish with plastic wrap and refrigerate for 1 hour.

Remove the chicken from the marinade with a slotted spoon. Heat the oil in a wok or skillet, and stir-fry the chicken and leek until the chicken is browned and the leek is beginning to soften.

Stir in the vegetables, ginger, and wine. Reduce the heat, cover and simmer for 5 minutes.

Place the sesame seeds on a cookie sheet under a hot broiler. Stir them once to make sure they toast evenly. Set aside to cool.

In a small bowl, combine the cornstarch with the water and whisk until smooth. Gradually add the liquid to the wok, stirring constantly until thickened.

Pile on a bed of hot rice and top with the sesame seeds, then serve.

chicken
& shiitake mushrooms

		ingredients	
very easy		MARINADE	1 tsp grated fresh root ginger
		scant 1 cup white sugar	3 carrots, sliced thinly
serves 4		225 ml/8 fl oz soy sauce	2 onions, sliced thinly
		1 tsp Chinese five spice powder	100 g/3½ oz beansprouts
		1 cup sweet sherry	4½ cups fresh or dried shiitake
			mushrooms, sliced thinly
10 minutes		STIR-FRY	3 tbsp chopped fresh cilantro
		2 tbsp vegetable oil	
		1½ lb/675 g chicken breast, skinned	cooked noodles, to serve
10 minutes		and cut into 1 inch/2.5 cm chunks	

Combine the sugar, soy sauce, Chinese five spice powder, and sweet sherry in a bowl. Mix well and set aside.

In a wok or skillet, heat the oil over a medium–high heat. Add the chicken and stir-fry for 2 minutes, then add the ginger and cook for 1 minute, stirring continuously. Add the soy sauce mixture and cook for 2 more minutes.

One at a time add the carrots, onions, beansprouts, mushrooms, and cilantro. Stir-fry after each addition.

Once the marinade has reduced and is thick, transfer the stir-fry to warm serving bowls. Serve hot with boiled noodles.

hot & spicy chicken
with peanuts

		ingredients	
	extremely easy	MARINADE 2 tbsp soy sauce 1 tsp chili powder (or to taste)	1 tsp grated fresh root ginger 3 shallots, sliced thinly 1½ cups carrots, sliced thinly 1 tsp white wine vinegar
	serves 4	STIR-FRY 12 oz/350 g chicken breasts, skinned and cut into chunks 4 tbsp peanut oil 1 clove garlic, chopped finely	pinch of sugar scant ⅔ cup roasted peanuts 1 tbsp peanut oil
	8 minutes +30 minutes to marinate		
	8 minutes		cooked noodles, to serve

Mix the soy sauce and chili powder in a bowl. Add the chicken chunks and toss to coat. Cover with plastic wrap and refrigerate for 30 minutes.

Heat the oil in a wok or skillet, and stir-fry the chicken until browned and well cooked. Remove from the wok then set aside and keep warm.

If necessary, add a little more oil to the wok, then add the garlic, ginger, shallots, and carrots. Stir-fry for 2–3 minutes.

Return the chicken to the wok and fry until it is warmed through. Add the vinegar, sugar, and peanuts, then stir well and drizzle with the peanut oil.

Serve immediately on a bed of noodles.

chicken fried rice

		ingredients
extremely easy		½ tbsp sesame oil 1 celery stalk, diced 6 shallots, peeled and cut into fourths 1 yellow bell pepper, diced 1 lb/450 g cooked, cubed 1½ cups fresh peas chicken meat 3½ oz/100 g canned corn 3 tbsp soy sauce 3⅔ cups cooked long-grain rice 2 carrots, diced 2 large eggs, scrambled
serves 4		
12 minutes		
12 minutes		

Heat the oil in a large skillet over a medium heat. Add the shallots and cook until soft, then add the chicken and 2 tablespoons of the soy sauce and stir-fry for 5–6 minutes.

Stir in the carrots, celery, yellow bell pepper, peas, and corn and stir-fry for another 5 minutes. Add the rice and stir thoroughly.

Finally, stir in the scrambled eggs and the remaining tablespoon of soy sauce. Serve immediately.

turkey with bamboo shoots & water chestnuts

		ingredients	
very easy		MARINADE	125 g/4½ oz small mushrooms,
		4 tbsp sweet sherry	cut into halves
serves 4		1 tbsp lemon juice	1 green bell pepper, cut into strips
		1 tbsp soy sauce	1 zucchini, sliced thinly
		2 tsp grated fresh root ginger	4 scallions, cut into fourths
11 minutes + 3–4 hours to marinate		1 clove garlic, crushed	4 oz/115 g canned bamboo shoots, drained
		STIR-FRY	4 oz/115 g canned sliced water
12 minutes		1 lb/450 g turkey breast, cubed	chestnuts, drained
		1 tbsp sesame oil	
		2 tbsp vegetable oil	cooked noodles, to serve

Blend the sherry, lemon juice, soy sauce, ginger, and garlic in a bowl, then add the turkey and stir. Cover the dish with plastic wrap and refrigerate to marinate for 3–4 hours.

In a wok or skillet, add the sesame oil and vegetable oil and heat slowly. Remove the chicken from the marinade with a slotted spoon (reserving the marinade) and stir-fry a few pieces at a time until browned. Remove the chicken from the wok and set aside.

Add the mushrooms, green bell pepper, and zucchini to the wok and stir-fry for 3 minutes. Add the scallions and stir-fry for 1 minute more. Add the bamboo shoots and water chestnuts to the wok, then the chicken along with half of the reserved marinade. Stir over a medium–high heat for another 2–3 minutes, or until the ingredients are evenly coated and the marinade has reduced.

Serve immediately over noodles or rice.

ginger shrimp
with oyster mushrooms

		ingredients	
	very easy	⅔ cup chicken bouillon	3 carrots, sliced thinly
		2 tsp sesame seeds	7 cups oyster mushrooms, sliced thinly
	serves 4	3 tsp grated fresh root ginger	1 large red bell pepper, sliced thinly
		1 tbsp soy sauce	1 lb/450 g large shrimp, shelled
		¼ tsp hot pepper sauce	2 garlic cloves, crushed
	10 minutes	1 tsp cornstarch	
		2 tbsp vegetable oil	cooked rice, to serve
	10 minutes		

In a small bowl, stir together the chicken bouillon, sesame seeds, ginger, soy sauce, hot pepper sauce, and cornstarch until well blended. Set aside.

In a large wok or skillet, heat 2 tablespoons of the oil. Stir-fry the carrots for 3 minutes, then remove from the wok and set aside.

Add 1 tablespoon more oil to the wok and cook the mushrooms for 2 minutes. Remove from the wok and set aside.

Add more oil if needed and stir-fry the bell pepper with the shrimp and garlic for 3 minutes, or until the shrimp turn pink and opaque.

Stir the sauce again and pour it into the wok. Cook until the mixture bubbles, then return the carrots and mushrooms to the wok. Cover and cook for 2 minutes more, or until heated through.

Serve over hot cooked rice.

fish
& seafood

Stir-frying is a great way to prepare fish and seafood because it enhances their delicate texture and subtle flavors. This selection includes spicy options such as Sweet Chili Squid and Ginger Shrimp with Oyster Mushrooms as well as dishes enhanced with herbs, such as Mixed Seafood & Asparagus and Salmon & Scallops with Cilantro and Lime— a range of recipes to suit every taste.

simple stir-fried scallops

		ingredients	
extremely easy		SAUCE	STIR-FRY
		2 tbsp lemon juice	1 lb/450 g scallops
		2 tbsp soy sauce	2 tbsp sesame oil
serves 4		1 tbsp honey	1 tbsp chopped fresh cilantro
		1 tbsp ground fresh root ginger	1 tbsp chopped flatleaf parsley
		1 tbsp fish sauce, optional	
5 minutes		1 clove garlic, peeled and flattened	rice noodles, to serve
6 minutes			

Combine the lemon juice, soy sauce, honey, ginger, fish sauce, and garlic in a bowl and stir well to dissolve the honey. Add the scallops and toss to coat.

Heat a wok or heavy skillet over the highest heat for 3 minutes. Add the oil and heat for 30 seconds.

Add the scallops with their sauce and the cilantro and parsley to the wok. Stir constantly, cooking for about 3 minutes (less time if the scallops are smaller).

Serve immediately over rice noodles.

shrimp, snow peas
& cashew nuts

		ingredients	
very easy		generous ½ cup dry roasted cashew nuts	1 clove of garlic, chopped coarsely
			450 g/1 lb uncooked shrimp, shelled
serves 4		3 tbsp peanut oil	1 tsp cornstarch
		4 scallions, slivered	2 tbsp soy sauce
		2 celery stalks, sliced thinly	¼ cup chicken bouillon
		3 carrots, sliced finely	2 cups savoy cabbage, shredded
12 minutes		100 g/3½ oz baby corn cobs, halved	1¾ cups snow peas
		3 cups mushrooms, sliced finely	
			cooked rice, to serve
9 minutes			

Put the skillet over a medium heat and add the cashew nuts; toast them until they begin to brown. Remove with a slotted spoon and reserve.

Add the oil to the pan and heat. Add the scallions, celery, carrots, and baby corn cobs and cook, stirring occasionally, over a medium–high heat for 3–4 minutes.

Add the mushrooms and cook until they become brown. Mix in the garlic and shrimp, stirring until the shrimp turn pink.

Mix the cornstarch smoothly with the soy sauce and chicken bouillon. Add the liquid to the shrimp mixture and stir. Then add the savoy cabbage, snow peas, and all but a few of the cashew nuts and cook for 2 minutes.

Garnish with the reserved cashew nuts and serve on a bed of rice.

mixed seafood
& asparagus

		ingredients	
easy		MARINADE	8 oz/225 g asparagus,
		4 tbsp sweet sherry	cut into 1 inch/2.5 cm pieces
serves 4		1 tsp cornstarch	4 oz/115 g baby corn cobs
			½ cup chicken bouillon
		STIR-FRY	2 tbsp sherry
10 minutes		8 oz/225 g shrimp, shelled	1 tsp sesame oil
+ 30 minutes		8 oz/225 g tuna,	½ tsp sugar
to marinate		cut into 2.5 cm/1 inch chunks	salt and pepper
		4 oz/115 g squid, sliced into strips	2 tsp cornstarch
8 minutes		2 tbsp peanut oil	5 tsp water
		1 clove garlic, crushed	cooked rice, to serve

To make the marinade, mix the sweet sherry and 1 teaspoon of
the cornstarch together in a large bowl, and season to taste. Add
the shrimp, tuna, and squid to the marinade and mix well to coat.
Cover with plastic wrap and refrigerate for 30 minutes.

Place a wok or skillet over a high heat until hot. Add the oil, then
stir-fry the garlic for about 10 seconds. Remove the seafood from
the marinade with a slotted spoon and add to the wok. Stir-fry for
2 minutes, then remove from the wok and set aside.

Add the asparagus, baby corn, and bouillon to the wok; cover and
cook for 2 minutes. Add the sherry, sesame oil, sugar, and salt and
pepper, then stir.

Return the seafood to the wok and heat through. Whisk together
2 teaspoons of cornstarch and the water. Add to the wok, stirring,
until the sauce boils and thickens. Serve on a bed of rice.

monkfish stir-fry

		ingredients
extremely easy	2 tsp sesame oil 1 lb/450 g monkfish steaks, cut into 1 inch/2.5 cm chunks 1 onion, sliced thinly	3 cups mushrooms, sliced thinly 2 tbsp soy sauce 1 tbsp lemon juice
serves 4	3 cloves garlic, chopped finely 1 tsp grated fresh ginger root	lemon wedges, to garnish
10 minutes	8 oz/225 g fine tip asparagus	cooked noodles, to serve
5 minutes		

Heat the oil in a skillet over a medium–high heat. Add the fish, onion, garlic, ginger, asparagus, and mushrooms. Stir-fry for 2–3 minutes.

Stir in the soy sauce and lemon juice and cook for another minute. Remove from the heat and transfer to warm serving dishes.

Garnish with lemon wedges and serve immediately on a bed of cooked noodles.

sweet chili squid

		ingredients	
extremely easy		1 tbsp sesame seeds, toasted	4 tbsp soy sauce
		2 tbsp sesame oil	1 tsp sugar
serves 4		10 oz/280 g squid, cut into strips	1 tsp hot chili flakes, or to taste
		2 red bell peppers, sliced thinly	1 clove of garlic, crushed
		3 shallots, sliced thinly	1 tsp sesame oil
		1½ cups mushrooms, sliced thinly	
10 minutes		1 tbsp dry sherry	cooked rice, to serve
7 minutes			

Place the sesame seeds on a cookie sheet and toast under a hot broiler, then set aside. Heat 1 tablespoon of oil in a skillet over a medium heat. Add the squid and cook for 2 minutes. Remove from the skillet and set aside.

Add the other tablespoon of oil to the skillet and cook the bell peppers and shallots over a medium heat for 1 minute. Add the mushrooms and cook for another 2 minutes.

Return the squid to the skillet and add the sherry, soy sauce, sugar, chili flakes, and garlic, stirring thoroughly. Cook for another 2 minutes.

Sprinkle with the toasted sesame seeds, then drizzle over the sesame oil and mix. Serve on a bed of rice.

salmon & scallops
with cilantro & lime

		ingredients	
very easy		6 tbsp peanut oil	1 clove garlic, crushed
		10 oz/280 g salmon steak, skinned	6 tbsp chopped fresh cilantro
serves 4		and cut into 2.5 cm/1 inch chunks	3 shallots, sliced thinly
		8 oz/225 g scallops	2 limes, juiced
		3 carrots, sliced thinly	1 tsp lime zest
		2 celery stalks, cut into	1 tsp dried red pepper flakes
12 minutes		1 inch/2.5 cm pieces	3 tbsp dry sherry
		2 orange bell peppers, sliced thinly	3 tbsp soy sauce
		3 cups oyster mushrooms,	
8 minutes		sliced thinly	cooked noodles, to serve

In a wok or large frying pan, heat the oil over a medium heat. Add the salmon and scallops, and stir-fry for 3 minutes. Remove from the pan, then set aside and keep warm.

Add the carrots, celery, bell peppers, mushrooms, and garlic to the wok and stir-fry for 3 minutes. Add the cilantro and shallots, and stir.

Add the lime juice and zest, dried red pepper flakes, sherry, and soy sauce and stir. Return the salmon and scallops to the wok and stir-fry carefully for another minute.

Serve immediately on a bed of cooked noodles.

beef
& pork

Stir-frying beef and pork is one of the
quickest ways of cooking these meats—
and one of the tastiest and healthiest, too.
If you favor Thai flavors, you can choose
Thai Marinated Beef with Celery. If you
prefer, you can choose Chinese dishes,
such as Szechuan-style Pork & Bell Pepper
or Chinese-style Marinated Beef with
Vegetables. But whatever your taste,
there's something here for everyone.

beef & peanuts
with vegetables

		ingredients	
very easy		MARINADE	1 clove garlic, crushed
		1 tsp cornstarch	½ cup water
serves 4		1 tbsp soy sauce	2 tbsp peanut oil
		1 tsp grated fresh root ginger	4 scallions, sliced thinly
			4 oz/115 g baby corn cobs, halved
8 minutes +20 minutes to marinate		STIR-FRY	1 carrot, sliced thinly
		1 lb/450 g rump steak, cut into thin strips	scant ⅔ cup roasted peanuts
		1 tsp cornstarch	fresh cilantro, to garnish
6 minutes		1 tbsp soy sauce	
		2 tsp white wine vinegar	cooked rice, to serve

To make the marinade, mix together the cornstarch, soy sauce, and ginger in a medium bowl. Add the beef strips and toss to coat well. Cover with plastic wrap and let marinate for 20 minutes.

In a small bowl, mix 1 teaspoon of cornstarch with 1 tablespoon of soy sauce, the wine vinegar, garlic, and the water and set aside.

In a wok or skillet, heat 1 tablespoon of oil over a medium heat. Stir-fry the beef for 2 minutes, then remove and set aside.

Using the same wok, heat the remaining oil, then add the scallions, corn cobs, and carrots and stir-fry for 2 minutes. Stir in the beef and soy sauce mixture and bring to a boil. When the stir-fry thickens, add the peanuts. Transfer the stir-fry to warm serving dishes and garnish with fresh cilantro. Serve on a bed of rice.

pork with basil & lemongrass

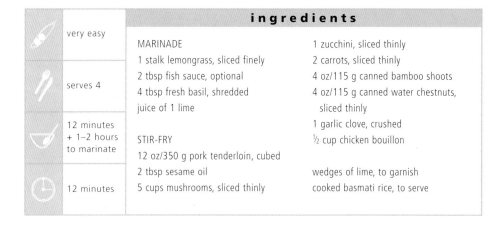

		ingredients
very easy	**MARINADE**	1 zucchini, sliced thinly
	1 stalk lemongrass, sliced finely	2 carrots, sliced thinly
serves 4	2 tbsp fish sauce, optional	4 oz/115 g canned bamboo shoots
	4 tbsp fresh basil, shredded	4 oz/115 g canned water chestnuts,
	juice of 1 lime	sliced thinly
12 minutes		1 garlic clove, crushed
+ 1–2 hours	**STIR-FRY**	½ cup chicken bouillon
to marinate	12 oz/350 g pork tenderloin, cubed	
	2 tbsp sesame oil	wedges of lime, to garnish
12 minutes	5 cups mushrooms, sliced thinly	cooked basmati rice, to serve

Mix the lemongrass, fish sauce (if desired), basil, and lime juice in a bowl. Stir in the pork and toss well to coat. Cover with plastic wrap and refrigerate for 1–2 hours.

Heat 1 tablespoon of the oil in a wok or skillet over a medium heat. Add the meat and the marinade and stir-fry until the pork is browned. Remove from the wok, set aside and keep warm.

Add the remaining 1 tablespoon of oil to the wok and heat. Add all the vegetables and the garlic and stir-fry for about 3 minutes.

Return the pork to the wok and add the chicken bouillon. Cook for 5 minutes, or until the bouillon is reduced.

Transfer the stir-fry to warm serving dishes and garnish with wedges of lime. Serve on a bed of basmati rice.

hot & spicy beef
with toasted pine nuts

		ingredients	
very easy		MARINADE	2 tbsp white wine vinegar
		2 tbsp soy sauce	1 tsp cornstarch
serves 4		1 tbsp cornstarch	2 tbsp peanut oil
		1 tbsp water	3 tsp grated fresh root ginger
			2 red, hot chiles, chopped finely
10 minutes + 1 hour to marinate		STIR-FRY	1 leek, sliced thinly
		1 lb/450 g rump steak, cut into thin strips	2 carrots, sliced thinly
			3½ oz/100 g fine tip asparagus
		⅓ cup pine nuts	3 shallots, sliced thinly
12 minutes		1 lime, juiced	
		1 tbsp soy sauce	cooked noodles, to serve

To make the marinade, mix the soy sauce with the cornstarch and water in a medium bowl. Add the beef and stir until the meat is well coated. Cover the bowl with plastic wrap and chill in the refrigerator for 1 hour. Spread the pine nuts on a cookie sheet and toast under a broiler.

Mix the lime juice, soy sauce, vinegar, cornstarch and 1 tablespoon of the peanut oil in a small bowl and set aside. Heat the remaining peanut oil in a wok or large skillet. Stir-fry the ginger, chiles, and leek for 2 minutes. Add the beef and the marinade and stir-fry for another minute.

Stir in the carrots, asparagus, and shallots and cook for 7 minutes, or until the beef is cooked through. Add the lime mixture, then reduce the heat and simmer until the liquid thickens. Remove from the heat and sprinkle with the pine nuts, then serve.

quick pork &
pasta stir-fry

		ingredients	
extremely easy		1 tbsp peanut oil	1 carrot, sliced thinly
		½ tsp chili powder, or to taste	1 zucchini, sliced thinly
serves 4		2 garlic cloves, crushed	12 oz/350 g pork tenderloin, cubed
		½ red cabbage, shredded	
		2 leeks, sliced thinly	cooked fettucine or vermicelli, to serve
8 minutes		1 orange bell pepper, sliced thinly	
8 minutes			

Heat the oil in a wok or large skillet over a medium heat and add the chili powder, garlic, and red cabbage. Stir-fry for 2–3 minutes.

Stir in the rest of the vegetables and cook for another 2 minutes. Add the meat, then increase the heat and stir-fry for 5 minutes, or until the pork is well cooked and the dish is piping hot.

Serve immediately over fettucine or vermicelli.

szechuan-style
pork & bell pepper

		ingredients	
very easy		MARINADE	1 cup water
		1 tbsp soy sauce	2 tbsp peanut oil
serves 4		pinch of chili flakes	2 leeks, sliced thinly
			1 red bell pepper, cut into thin strips
		STIR-FRY	1 zucchini, cut into thin strips
10 minutes +30 minutes to marinate		1 lb 2 oz/500 g pork tenderloin, cubed	1 carrot, cut into thin strips
		2 tbsp cornstarch	pinch of salt
		3 tbsp soy sauce	
12 minutes		1 tbsp white wine vinegar	cooked wild rice, to serve

To make the marinade, mix the soy sauce and chili flakes in a bowl. Add the pork cubes and toss to coat. Cover with plastic wrap and let stand for 30 minutes.

Combine the cornstarch, soy sauce, and white wine vinegar in a small bowl. Stir in the water gradually, then set aside.

Heat 1 tablespoon of the oil in a wok or skillet. Add the pork and marinade mixture and stir-fry for 2–3 minutes. Remove the pork from the wok with a slotted spoon and set aside.

Heat the remaining oil in the wok, then add the leeks and red bell pepper and stir-fry for 2 minutes. Next, add the zucchini, carrot, and salt and stir-fry for 2 more minutes.

Stir in the pork and the cornstarch mixture and bring to a boil, stirring constantly until the sauce thickens. Remove from the heat.

Serve immediately over cooked wild rice.

ginger beef with
yellow bell peppers

		ingredients	
extremely easy		MARINADE	2 garlic cloves, crushed
		2 tbsp soy sauce	2 tbsp grated fresh root ginger
serves 4		2 tsp peanut oil	pinch of chili flakes
		1½ tsp superfine sugar	2 yellow bell peppers, sliced thinly
		1 tsp cornstarch	4½ oz/125 g baby corn
10 minutes + 30 minutes to marinate			1¾ cups snow peas
		STIR-FRY	
		1 lb 2 oz/500 g beef fillet, cut into 1 inch/2.5 cm cubes	hot noodles drizzled with sesame oil, to serve
9 minutes		2 tsp peanut oil	

To make the marinade, mix the soy sauce, peanut oil, sugar, and cornstarch in a bowl. Stir in the beef cubes, then cover with plastic wrap and set aside to marinate for 30 minutes.

Heat the peanut oil in a wok or skillet over a medium heat. Add the garlic, ginger, and chili flakes and cook for 30 seconds. Stir in the yellow bell peppers and baby corn, and stir-fry for 2 minutes. Add the snow peas and cook for another minute.

Remove the vegetables from the wok. Put the beef cubes and marinade into the wok and stir-fry for 3–4 minutes, or until cooked to taste. Return the vegetables to the wok and mix well, then cook until all the ingredients are heated through.

Remove from the heat and serve over noodles.

chinese-style marinated beef with vegetables

		ingredients	
easy		MARINADE	3 tbsp sesame oil
		1 tbsp dry sherry	½ tbsp cornstarch
serves 4		½ tbsp soy sauce	½ tbsp soy sauce
		½ tbsp cornstarch	3 tbsp sesame oil
		½ tsp superfine sugar	1 head of broccoli, cut into florets
12 minutes +30 minutes to marinate		2 garlic cloves, chopped finely	2 carrots, cut into thin strips
		1 tbsp sesame oil	1¼ cups snow peas
			½ cup beef bouillon
		STIR-FRY	9 oz/250 g baby spinach, shredded
6 minutes		1 lb 2 oz/500 g rump steak,	fresh cilantro, to garnish
		cut into thin strips	cooked white rice or noodles, to serve

To make the marinade, mix the sherry, soy sauce, cornstarch, sugar, garlic, and sesame oil in a bowl. Add the beef to the mixture, cover with plastic wrap and let marinate for 30 minutes.

Heat 1 tablespoon of the sesame oil in a wok or skillet. Stir-fry the beef without its marinade for 2 minutes, or until medium-rare. Discard the marinade. Remove the beef from the wok and set aside.

Combine the cornstarch and soy sauce in a bowl and set aside. Pour the remaining 2 tablespoons of sesame oil into the wok, add the broccoli, carrots, and snow peas and stir-fry for 2 minutes.

Add the bouillon, then cover the pan and steam for one minute. Stir in the spinach, beef, and the cornstarch mixture. Cook until the juices boil and thicken.

Serve over white rice or noodles and garnish with fresh cilantro.

hot sesame beef

	very easy	
	serves 4	
	10 minutes	
	10 minutes	

ingredients

1 lb 2 oz/500 g beef fillet,
  cut into thin strips
1½ tbsp sesame seeds
½ cup beef bouillon
2 tbsp soy sauce
2 tbsp grated fresh root ginger
2 garlic cloves, chopped finely
1 tsp cornstarch
½ tsp chili flakes
3 tbsp sesame oil

1 large head of broccoli,
  cut into florets
1 orange bell pepper, sliced thinly
1 red chile, seeded and sliced finely
1 tbsp chili oil, to taste

1 tbsp chopped fresh cilantro,
  to garnish

cooked wild rice, to serve

Mix the beef strips with 1 tablespoon of the sesame seeds in a small bowl. In a separate bowl, whisk together the beef bouillon, soy sauce, ginger, garlic, cornstarch and chili flakes.

Heat 1 tablespoon of the sesame oil in a wok or large skillet. Stir-fry the beef strips for 2–3 minutes. Remove and set aside.

Discard any oil remaining in the wok, then wipe with paper towels to remove any stray sesame seeds. Heat the remaining oil and add the broccoli, orange bell pepper, chile and chili oil (if desired), then stir-fry for 2–3 minutes. Stir in the beef bouillon mixture, then cover and simmer for 2 minutes.

Return the beef to the wok and simmer until the juices thicken, stirring occasionally. Cook for another 1–2 minutes.

Sprinkle with the remaining sesame seeds. Serve over cooked wild rice and garnish with fresh cilantro.

beef with cashew nuts

		ingredients	
easy		4 tbsp peanut oil	4 tsp soy sauce
		1 lb 2 oz/500 g beef fillet,	1 tsp sesame oil
		cut into 1 inch/2.5 cm cubes	1 tbsp oyster sauce
serves 4		8 scallions, trimmed and sliced	1 tsp chili sauce
		2 carrots, cut into thin strips	
		8 radishes, sliced thinly	GARNISH
12 minutes		2 garlic cloves, chopped finely	2 tbsp cashew nuts
		2 tbsp grated fresh root ginger	1 tbsp chopped fresh cilantro
		scant ⅔ cup cashew nuts	
9 minutes		½ cup water	cooked noodles or rice, to serve
		4 tsp cornstarch	

In a wok or skillet, heat 2 tablespoons of the peanut oil and stir-fry the beef cubes for 3–4 minutes. Cooking the meat in batches can help to speed up the process. Remove the cooked meat from the wok and set aside.

Heat the remaining 2 tablespoons of peanut oil in the wok and stir-fry the scallions, carrots, radishes, garlic, ginger, and cashew nuts for 1–2 minutes.

Mix the water, cornstarch, soy sauce, sesame oil, oyster sauce, and chili sauce in a small jug or bowl and set aside.

Return the beef to the wok and stir-fry until hot; then pour the cornstarch mixture into the wok. Cook gently, stirring constantly until the sauce boils and thickens.

Remove from the heat and pile on top of the rice or noodles, then garnish with cashew nuts and cilantro.

beef & black
bean sauce

	ingredients	
extremely easy	**MARINADE**	**STIR-FRY**
	1 tbsp soy sauce	13 oz/375 g rump steak, cubed
	1 tbsp dry sherry	6 tbsp vegetable oil
serves 4	2 tbsp water	4 cloves garlic, chopped finely
	1 tbsp cornstarch	1 tbsp grated fresh root ginger
12 minutes + 30 minutes to marinate	**SAUCE**	2 leeks, sliced thinly
	2 tbsp black bean sauce	1 head of broccoli, cut into florets
	1 tbsp soy sauce	1 head of cauliflower, cut into florets
12 minutes	1 tbsp dry sherry	4 tbsp water
	1 tbsp cornstarch	
		cooked noodles or rice, to serve

To make the marinade, combine the soy sauce, sherry, water, and cornstarch in a bowl. Add the cubes of beef and stir to coat well, then set aside to marinate for 30 minutes. In a separate bowl, mix the sauce ingredients together.

In a wok or skillet, heat 4 tablespoons of the oil and stir-fry the beef for 3–4 minutes. Remove from the wok and set aside.

Wipe the wok clean with paper towels. Heat the remaining oil, and stir-fry the garlic, ginger and leeks for 1 minute. Add the broccoli, cauliflower, and water. Reduce the heat, then cover the wok and simmer for 3–4 minutes.

Return the beef to the wok and stir well. Pour the sauce into the wok and bring to a boil. Reduce the heat and simmer for 4–5 minutes, or until the sauce is thick and the ingredients are cooked to your liking. Serve over cooked noodles or rice.

marinated steak
with rice noodles

		ingredients	
	easy	MARINADE	STIR-FRY
		1 tsp dry sherry	10 oz/280 g rump steak, cut into strips
	serves 4	1 tbsp soy sauce	1¼ cups vegetable oil,
		1 tbsp peanut oil	to deep-fry noodles
		1 tsp sesame oil	3 cups rice noodles
	8 minutes	1 tsp cornstarch	1 tbsp soy sauce
	+ 1 hour	2 tsp honey	1 tbsp black bean sauce
	to marinate	1 shallot, chopped finely	1 tsp cornstarch
			½ cup water
	8 minutes		8 scallions, sliced thinly
			fresh cilantro, to garnish

For the marinade, mix the sherry, soy sauce, peanut oil, sesame oil, cornstarch, honey and shallot in a bowl. Add the beef and toss to coat. Cover with plastic wrap and refrigerate for 1 hour.

In a wok or skillet, heat the oil over a high heat until very hot. Using a metal sieve, lower the noodles into the oil for 3 seconds until they are puffed up. Remove carefully, then let the oil drain from the strainer and set the noodles aside to cool on paper towels. Snap the noodles into smaller lengths and set aside.

Take 5 tablespoons of oil from the wok and heat in a second wok or skillet. Stir-fry the beef over a medium heat for 3–4 minutes. Remove from the wok and set aside. Add the soy sauce, black bean sauce, cornstarch and water to the oil in the second wok and cook gently until the mixture boils. Add the scallions and beef and cook for 1 minute. Remove from the heat and serve over the noodles. Garnish with cilantro.

thai marinated beef
with celery

		ingredients	
extremely easy		MARINADE	1 red bell pepper, cut into thin strips
		1 tsp salt	1 red chile, seeds removed,
serves 4		2 tbsp fish sauce	sliced finely
			1 cup vegetable oil
		STIR-FRY	
10 minutes + 1 hour to marinate		1 lb 2 oz/500 g beef fillet, cut into thin strips	cooked rice noodles drizzled with sesame oil, to serve
		3 celery stalks, cut into 1 inch/2.5 cm batons	
6 minutes			

To make the marinade, mix the salt and fish sauce in a large bowl. Add the beef and toss to coat. Cover with plastic wrap and put in the refrigerator for 1 hour to marinate.

Heat the oil in a wok and deep-fry the beef over a medium heat for 2–3 minutes, or until crispy. Remove the wok from the heat and, using a slotted spoon, lift out the meat and drain it on paper towels. Discard all but 2 tablespoons of the oil.

Heat the remaining oil in the wok and stir-fry the celery, red bell pepper and chile for 1 minute. Add the beef and cook until hot.

Serve over noodles drizzled with sesame oil.

stir-fry solo

		ingredients	
easy		MARINADE	1 small head of broccoli, cut into florets
		1 tsp cornstarch	
serves 1		2 tbsp dry sherry	1 celery stalk, cut into batons
			1 carrot, cut into batons
		STIR-FRY	¼ orange bell pepper, sliced thinly
10 minutes +30 minutes to marinate		4½ oz/125 g chicken breast, cut into thin strips	2 tbsp soy sauce
		2 tsp sesame oil	1 tbsp chopped fresh cilantro, to garnish
8 minutes		2 garlic cloves, crushed	
		1 tsp grated fresh root ginger	cooked rice, to serve

To make the marinade, combine the cornstarch and dry sherry in a bowl. Add the chicken, tossing well to coat. Cover with plastic wrap and let marinate in the refrigerator for 30 minutes.

Put the oil in a wok or large skillet and heat over a high heat. Add the garlic, ginger, and chicken and cook for 3 minutes.

Add the broccoli, celery, carrot, and bell pepper to the wok and cook for 3 minutes, stirring constantly. Add more oil if necessary to prevent the dish drying out. Stir in the soy sauce and cook for another minute.

Serve piled on a bed of rice and garnished with the cilantro.

pad thai
(thai fried noodles)

		ingredients		
easy	3 cups rice noodles	vegetable oil,	125 g/4½ oz snow peas	
	generous ½ cup peanuts,	for deep frying	175 g/6 oz shrimp, shelled,	
serves 4	chopped coarsely	3 tbsp peanut oil	then cut in half lengthwise	
	2 tbsp lime juice	1 garlic clove, crushed	3 eggs, beaten	
	1 tbsp superfine sugar	1 onion, sliced finely		
15 minutes	6 tbsp fish sauce	1 red bell pepper,	GARNISH	
+20 minutes to soak noodles	1 tsp hot chili sauce,	sliced thinly	1 lemon, cut into wedges	
	or to taste	9 oz/250 g chicken breast,	4 scallions, chopped finely	
	250 g/9 oz firm bean	cut into thin strips	2 tbsp chopped peanuts	
14 minutes	curd, cubed	90 g/3 oz beansprouts	1 tbsp chopped fresh basil	

Soak the noodles in a bowl of warm water for about 20 minutes. Drain in a colander and set aside. In a bowl, combine the peanuts, lime juice, sugar, fish sauce, and hot chili sauce and set aside.

Rinse the bean curd in cold water, then place between layers of paper towels and pat dry. Heat the oil for deep-frying in a large wok or skillet. Deep-fry the bean curd over a medium heat for 2 minutes, or until light brown and crisp. Remove from the heat, lift the bean curd out with a slotted spoon and set aside on paper towels to drain.

Heat a large wok or skillet and add the peanut oil, garlic, onion, red bell pepper, and chicken strips. Cook for 2–3 minutes. Stir in the beansprouts and snow peas and cook for 1 minute. Then add the shrimp, noodles, eggs, and bean curd and stir-fry for 4–5 minutes. Add the peanut and lime juice mixture and cook for 3–4 minutes. Transfer to warm dishes and garnish, then serve.

vegetable dishes

Vegetables retain their crunchy freshness when they are stir-fried, and their natural healthy taste can be quickly enhanced with delicious simple and exotic sauces.

From Oyster Mushrooms & Vegetables with Peanut Chili Sauce and Spicy Indian Vegetarian Stir-fry through to Meatless Pad Thai, there is a great selection of main and side dishes here to tantalize all taste buds.

oyster mushrooms & vegetables with peanut chili sauce

		ingredients	
![] very easy		1 tbsp sesame oil	2 tbsp coarse peanut butter
		4 scallions, sliced finely	1 tsp chili powder, or to taste
serves 4		1 carrot, cut into batons	3 tbsp water
		1 zucchini, cut into batons	
		½ head of broccoli, cut into florets	wedges of lime, to garnish
10 minutes		9 cups oyster mushrooms, sliced thinly	cooked rice or noodles, to serve
6 minutes			

Heat the oil in a wok or skillet until almost smoking. Stir-fry the scallions for 1 minute. Add the carrot and zucchini and stir-fry for another minute. Then add the broccoli and cook for one more minute.

Stir in the mushrooms and cook until they are soft and at least half the liquid they produce has evaporated. Add the peanut butter and stir well. Season with the chili powder to taste. Finally, add the water and cook for one more minute.

Serve over rice or noodles and garnish with wedges of lime.

spicy indian
vegetarian stir-fry

		ingredients	
very easy		3 tbsp vegetable oil	¼ tsp chili powder
		½ tsp turmeric	4 tomatoes, chopped coarsely
serves 4		8 oz/225 g potatoes, cut into ½ inch/1 cm cubes	10½ oz/300 g spinach (de-stalked), chopped coarsely
		3 shallots, chopped finely	1¼ cups fresh or frozen peas
10 minutes		1 bay leaf	1 tbsp lemon juice
		½ tsp ground cumin	salt and pepper
		1 tsp finely grated fresh root ginger	
15 minutes			cooked basmati rice, to serve

In a wok or large skillet, heat 2 tablespoons of the oil and add the turmeric and a pinch of salt. Carefully add the potatoes, stirring continuously to coat in the turmeric. Stir-fry for 5 minutes, then remove from the wok and set aside.

Heat the remaining tablespoon of oil and stir-fry the shallots for 1–2 minutes. Mix in the bay leaf, cumin, ginger, and chili powder, then add the tomatoes and stir-fry for two minutes.

Add the spinach, mixing well to combine all the flavors. Cover and simmer for 2–3 minutes. Return the potatoes to the wok and add the peas and lemon juice. Cook for 5 minutes, or until the potatoes are tender.

Remove the wok from the heat and discard the bay leaf, then season with salt and pepper. Serve with cooked basmati rice.

classic stir-fried vegetables

		ingredients	
very easy	3 tbsp sesame oil	6 oz/175 g portobello or large cup
	8 scallions, chopped finely	mushrooms, sliced thinly
serves 4	1 garlic clove, crushed	7 oz/200 g fresh beansprouts
	1 tbsp grated fresh root ginger	9 oz/250 g canned water chestnuts,
	1 head of broccoli, cut into florets	drained
	1 orange or yellow bell pepper,	4 tsp soy sauce
10 minutes	chopped coarsely	
	125 g/4½ oz red cabbage, shredded	cooked wild rice, to serve
	125 g/4½ oz baby corn	
6 minutes		

Heat 2 tablespoons of the oil in a wok or large skillet over a high heat. Stir-fry six of the scallions, with the garlic and ginger for 30 seconds.

Add the broccoli, bell pepper, and red cabbage and stir-fry for 1–2 minutes. Mix in the baby corn and mushrooms and stir-fry for another 1–2 minutes.

Finally, add the beansprouts and water chestnuts and cook for another 2 minutes. Pour in the soy sauce to taste and stir well.

Transfer to warm dishes and serve immediately over cooked wild rice, and garnish with scallions.

squash & zucchini stir-fry

		ingredients	
very easy		1 butternut squash, peeled, seeded and cut into 1 inch/2.5 cm cubes	¼ small cauliflower, cut into florets
serves 4		2 tbsp olive oil	1 tsp chopped fresh basil
		2 tbsp vegetable oil	½ tsp dried oregano
		2 cloves of garlic, crushed	4 tbsp dry white wine
12 minutes		1 carrot, sliced thinly	1 tbsp chopped fresh cilantro
		2 green or yellow zucchini, sliced thinly on the diagonal	1 tbsp lemon juice
35 minutes		1 small head of broccoli, cut into florets	cooked noodles, to serve

Preheat the oven to 350°F/180°C. Place the butternut squash in an ovenproof dish and drizzle with the olive oil, then season generously. Bake for 20–30 minutes until firm but tender. Insert a knife into a squash cube to test for tenderness. Remove from the oven and set aside.

Heat the vegetable oil in a wok or large skillet. Add the garlic and cook for 30 seconds, then add the carrot, zucchini, broccoli and cauliflower. Stir-fry for 1 minute and then add the squash.

Add the basil, oregano and wine. Cover the wok and simmer for 3–4 minutes. Remove from the heat. Add the cilantro and the lemon juice. Serve immediately over cooked noodles.

spicy bean curd

		ingredients	
	very easy	MARINADE	4 tbsp peanut oil
		75 ml/2½ fl oz vegetable bouillon	1 tbsp grated fresh root ginger
	serves 4	2 tsp cornstarch	3 garlic cloves, crushed
		2 tbsp soy sauce	4 scallions, sliced thinly
		1 tbsp superfine sugar	1 head of broccoli, cut into florets
	10 minutes	pinch of chili flakes	1 carrot, cut into batons
	+20 minutes		1 yellow bell pepper, sliced thinly
	to marinate	STIR-FRY	5 cups shiitake mushrooms,
		9 oz/250 g firm bean curd, rinsed and	sliced thinly
	10 minutes	drained thoroughly and cut into	steamed rice, to serve
		½ inch/1 cm cubes	

Blend the vegetable bouillon, cornstarch, soy sauce, sugar, and chili flakes together in a large bowl. Add the bean curd and toss well to coat. Set aside to marinate for 20 minutes.

In a wok or large skillet, heat 2 tablespoons of the peanut oil and stir-fry the bean curd with its marinade until brown and crispy. Remove from the wok and set aside.

Heat the remaining 2 tablespoons of peanut oil in the wok and stir-fry the ginger, garlic, and scallions for 30 seconds. Add the broccoli, carrot, yellow bell pepper, and mushrooms to the wok and cook for 5–6 minutes. Return the bean curd to the wok and stir-fry to reheat. Serve immediately over steamed rice.

meatless pad thai (thai fried noodles)

		ingredients	
easy	5 cups rice noodles	4 tbsp sesame oil
	scant ⅔ cup peanuts, chopped coarsely	4 garlic cloves, crushed
serves 4		2 carrots, peeled and grated coarsely
	3 tbsp fresh lime juice	2 eggs, beaten
	3 tbsp tomato ketchup	6 scallions, sliced finely
12 minutes +20 minutes to soak noodles	1 tbsp light muscovado sugar	100 g/3½ oz fresh beansprouts
	2 tbsp soy sauce	GARNISH
	1 tsp hot chili sauce, or to taste	2 limes, cut into fourths
	250 g/9 oz firm bean curd, cubed	4 tbsp chopped fresh cilantro
12 minutes	vegetable oil, for deep-frying	

Soak the noodles in a bowl of warm water for about 20 minutes. Drain and set aside. In a small bowl, mix the peanuts, lime juice, ketchup, sugar, soy sauce, and hot chili sauce and set aside.

Put the noodles in boiling water and cook until the water starts to boil again. Remove, then drain and set aside. Rinse the bean curd, then place between paper towels and pat dry. Heat the vegetable oil in a wok and deep-fry the bean curd on a medium heat for 2 minutes until light brown. Remove from the heat, lift out the bean curd and place on paper towels to drain. Discard the oil.

Heat the sesame oil in the wok. Add the garlic and carrots and cook for 1 minute. Add the noodles and toss to coat. Add the peanut mixture and boil; stir until the liquid is absorbed. Move the noodles to the side of the wok. Add the eggs and scramble, then mix with the noodles. Add the scallions, beansprouts, and bean curd and stir-fry for 2 minutes. Remove from the heat, garnish and serve.

stir-fried asparagus & oyster mushrooms

		ingredients	
	extremely easy	1 lb 2 oz/500 g asparagus, cut into 1 inch/2.5 cm pieces	pinch of chili flakes
		½ cup chicken bouillon	salt and pepper, to taste
	serves 4	1 tbsp cornstarch	GARNISH
		1 tbsp water	1 tbsp chopped fresh parsley
		2 tbsp vegetable oil	1 tsp chopped fresh chives
	8 minutes	5 cups oyster mushrooms, sliced thinly	
	10 minutes		

Steam the asparagus for 4–6 minutes until tender and set aside. Combine the chicken bouillon, cornstarch and water in a small bowl and set aside.

Heat the oil in a wok or large skillet over a medium heat. Stir-fry the asparagus, mushrooms, and chili flakes for 1–2 minutes. Stir in the chicken bouillon and bring to a boil. Reduce the heat, add the cornstarch mixture and cook, stirring constantly for 2–3 minutes, or until thick.

Remove from the heat. Season to taste, then garnish with the parsley and chives and serve immediately.

red cabbage
& green beans

		ingredients
extremely easy		9 oz/250 g fine green beans
		1 tsp sesame oil
serves 4 (as a side dish)		1 onion, chopped finely
		3 carrots, cut into batons
		½ head red cabbage, shredded
8 minutes		5 tbsp vegetable bouillon
		2 tbsp soy sauce
14 minutes		

Boil a pan of water and blanch the green beans for 2–3 minutes. Remove from the heat, then drain and plunge into ice-cold water.

In a wok or large skillet, heat the oil and stir-fry the onion for 2 minutes. Add the carrots and cook for 3 minutes. Then mix in the green beans and stir-fry for 2 minutes. Finally, add the red cabbage and cook for 2 more minutes.

Pour in the vegetable bouillon and bring to a boil. Reduce the heat, then cover and simmer for 3–4 minutes. Add the soy sauce.

Transfer to warm dishes and serve immediately.

garlic spinach

		ingredients	
	extremely easy	6 tbsp vegetable oil 6 garlic cloves, crushed 2 tbsp black bean sauce 3 tomatoes, chopped coarsely 900 g/2 lb spinach, destalked and chopped roughly	1 tsp chili sauce, or to taste 2 tbsp lemon juice salt and pepper
	serves 4 as a side dish		
	6 minutes		
	4 minutes		

In a wok or large skillet, heat the oil and stir-fry the garlic, black bean sauce, and tomatoes for 1 minute. Stir in the spinach, chili sauce, and lemon juice and mix well. Cook for 3 minutes, or until the spinach is just wilted. Season to taste.

Remove from the heat and serve immediately.

stir-fried broccoli

extremely easy	**ingredients**	
serves 4 as a side dish	2 tbsp vegetable oil 2 medium heads of broccoli, 　cut into florets 2 tbsp soy sauce 1 tsp cornstarch 1 tbsp superfine sugar	1 tsp grated fresh root ginger 1 garlic clove, crushed pinch of hot chili flakes 1 tsp toasted sesame seeds, 　to garnish
8 minutes		
8 minutes		

In a wok or large skillet, heat the oil until almost smoking. Stir-fry the broccoli for 4–5 minutes.

In a small bowl, combine the soy sauce, cornstarch, sugar, ginger, garlic, and hot chili flakes. Add the mixture to the broccoli. Cook over a gentle heat, stirring constantly, for 2–3 minutes until the sauce thickens slightly.

Transfer to a serving dish, then garnish with the sesame seeds and serve immediately.

eggplant stir-fry

very easy	**ingredients**	
	2 eggplants	½ tsp paprika
serves 4 (as a side dish)	3 tbsp vegetable oil	¼ tsp ground cumin
	1 head of broccoli, cut into florets	3 tbsp water
6 minutes + 20 minutes to prepare eggplants	3 tomatoes, chopped coarsely	2 tbsp chopped fresh cilantro,
	1 tsp salt	to garnish
12 minutes		

Trim the eggplants and cut into 1 inch/2.5 cm cubes. Place in a bowl and sprinkle with salt, then set aside for 20 minutes to remove any bitter juices. Rinse and drain thoroughly.

In a wok or skillet, heat 2 tablespoons of the oil until it is nearly smoking. Add the eggplant and stir-fry for 2–3 minutes. Remove from the heat and transfer to paper towels using a slotted spoon.

Heat the remaining tablespoon of oil in the wok and stir-fry the broccoli over a medium heat for 2–3 minutes. Add the tomatoes and salt and cook for another 2 minutes. Stir in the paprika, cumin, water, and cooked eggplant and mix together thoroughly. Reduce the heat, then cover the wok and simmer for 5 minutes.

Remove from the heat, then garnish with the cilantro and serve.

index